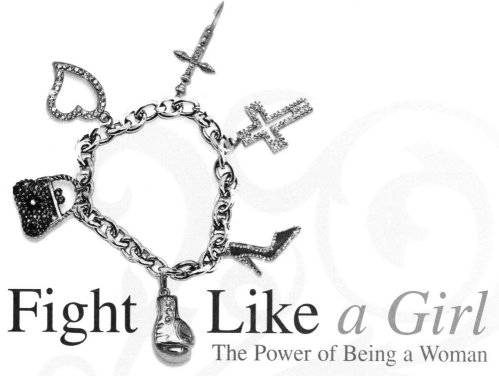

Fight *Like a Girl*

The Power of Being a Woman

Workbook

Lisa Bevere

ISBN 1-933185-07-4

Requests for information should be addressed to:
Messenger International
P. O. Box 888, Palmer Lake, CO 80133-0888
www.messengerintl.org

COVER, INTERIOR DESIGN & PRINTING:
Eastco Multi Media Solutions, Inc
3646 California Rd.
Orchard Park, NY 14127
www.eastcomultimedia.com

Co-Author: Heather Gemmen
Editor: Mary McNeil
Design Manager: Aaron La Porta
Designer: Heather Wierowski

Printed in Canada

Table of Contents

Instructions

We have designed this workbook to be an interactive approach to the truths found in *Fight Like a Girl*. The goal is to connect you with God's living Word so it will become flesh in your life and bring freedom. This workbook is perfect for both individual and group study.

Fight Like a Girl Curriculum

We have compiled a complete curriculum kit including: 12 video lessons on 4 DVD's, the *Fight Like a Girl* hardback book, and a corresponding 16 chapter interactive workbook. The 12 video sessions highlight the concepts found in the *Fight Like a Girl* book, while the interactive *Fight Like a Girl* workbook directly correlates to each chapter of the book.

We recommend using this curriculum as either a 12 or 16 week study. For a **12-week** study, there are 3 weeks in which multiple chapters should be completed. Based on the video sessions, we recommend grouping the following chapters in the book and workbook together to accompany the sessions:

- Chapters 3 and 4 with video session 3
- Chapters 8 and 9 with video session 7
- And Chapters 11, 12 and 13 with video session 9

For a **16-week** study there will be 4 weeks without a video session. For those 4 weeks, we recommend viewing the video session and completing one chapter in the workbook the first week. For the following week(s) discuss the additional chapter(s) without a video session.

- Video session 3 covers chapters 3 and 4 in the book and workbook.
- Video session 7 covers chapters 8 and 9 in the book and workbook.
- Video session 9 covers chapters 11, 12 and 13 in the book and workbook.

We pray you are blessed by this curriculum as you discover the truths of God!

Please feel free to contact our office if you have any questions. Our Church Relations team is available to assist you with any of our award winning curriculums. Also, please visit us on the web at www.messengerintl.org.

Beautiful Daughter *of the Most High God,*

Your time *of recovery is at hand. You hold*

the **power** *of ancient* **truths** *and faithful* **weapons** *which*

cannot fail, because they were forged in love.

Embrace *wisdom, courage and beauty. Reveal heaven's*

splendor *in the daughter you were created to be, for the*

women of the earth need you.

Lisa Bevere

You Fight Like a Girl!

1

Read chapter 1 of *Fight Like a Girl* and view DVD session 1.

What would fighting like a girl look like if it was done right?

> ### *Insight*
>
> I am not advocating we dumb it down or fake something we are not. I do think we need to ask *why* it is an insult to fight like a girl. Even better, I want girls and women to consider themselves *complimented* if they are told they fight like one.

LOCATE YOURSELF

What Kind of Fighter am I?

1. If my child were maliciously ridiculed by a teacher, I would
    A. shrug.
    B. move to a new district.
    C. meet with the teacher myself.
    D. tell my child to stand up for him or herself.

2. If the man I love forgot my birthday, I would
    A. forget about it myself.
    B. ignore him without saying why.
    C. tell him I was hurt and give him an opportunity to make up for it.
    D. threaten him in anger.

3. If my employer cut my wages without informing me, I would
   A. wonder what I did to deserve it, but never speak up.
   B. grumble to my friends.
   C. ask my boss for an explanation.
   D. reduce my level of work according to my diminished pay.

4. If I caught my best friend talking behind my back, I would
   A. accept that that is just the way she is.
   B. slink away and cry.
   C. ask her directly about her concerns.
   D. spread gossip that told my side of the story.

SCORE
If you selected mostly As, ask God to reveal His identity in you.
If you selected mostly Bs, you see the injustice around you, but you're motivated by fear.
If you selected mostly Cs, your sense of justice is balanced with a healthy dose of wisdom-way to fight like a girl.
If you selected mostly Ds, you know how to fight; just don't let anger rule you.

1. How do current and historical views of our gender affect how women engage in conflict? According to society, what does it look like to fight like a girl?

_____

_____

_____

_____

_____

_____

BIG *Idea*

If someone tells you you're fighting like a girl, that person likely means to insult you. But the truth is, girls were meant to fight like girls. For some odd reason though, most of us would rather be told we fight like men. Could this be because girls have developed the habit of fighting dirty? (p. 1)

_____

_____

_____

_____

2. Do you think most women prefer to be told they fight like men? Why or why not?

_____

_____

_____

_____

_____

_____

_____

_____

3. What is the strength of women, and how does that affect the way women should fight? Is there a right way for a woman to fight?

_____

_____

_____

_____

_____

_____

_____

_____

4. For what purpose were women originally created? (pp. 2-3)

_____

_____

_____

_____

_____

_____

_____

5. Do you think it's wrong for women to fight? Should women leave the fighting to men? Why or why not?

_____

_____

_____

_____

_____

_____

_____

_____

_____

_____

_____

With the fall everything changed (fill in the blank) (p. 3)

Dominion became _____

Multiplication became _____

Order spiraled into _____

6. The last to be created became the _____ in conflict. (p. 3)

ACTIVITY
Top Ten

Leader: Bring a stack of different types of magazines.

Grab a magazine or two from the stack and browse through, looking for issues worth fighting for—and issues not worth fighting for. After ten minutes or so, regroup to share your findings. Name the top-ten crucial issues worth fighting for—and, for fun, the top-ten frivolous issues. Choose an issue that seems to matter to everyone and consider adopting this as your group's main battle to tackle as you study *Fight Like a Girl* together. Research the topic further, pray over it regularly, and make a plan of action for battling.

BIG *Idea*

Enmity does not equate with the term "irreconcilable differences" we are so accustomed to hearing cited in divorce proceedings, but rather "irreconcilable *hostility*." This speaks of a hatred so profound, it is destined to not only exist perpetually, but to deepen and expand without end. (pp. 3-4)

ENMITY

←— PAST   FUTURE —→

•

CREATION
And I will put enmity
between you and the woman.
(Genesis 3:15 NIV)

REVELATION
Then the dragon became angry
at the woman, and he declared
war against the rest of her
children-all who keep God's
commandments and confess
that they belong to Jesus.
(Revelation 12:17 NLT)

7. What is the difference between irreconcilable differences and the hostilities between women and Satan? Is it just a matter of degree? Why or why not? (P. 3-4)

_____

_____

_____

_____

_____

_____

_____

_____

BIG *Idea*

Far too often when deception speaks, men and women both forget who they are and who their true allies are. The man's position is not up for grabs, just as it is not his to give away. The woman's place is not the man's for the taking, nor is it hers to forfeit. The two must stand together in their respective roles.

_____

_____

_____

_____

_____

8. Who is woman's true enemy? Considering who our enemy is—and who sets hostility between us—reconsider the question of whether a woman should fight. If we do not fight, what will happen?

---

9. How has Satan tricked men and women into thinking of each other as the enemy? How does Satan divide and conquer humans today?

---

10. What do you lose by grasping at something you are not meant to have? Describe a time you moved outside God's wisdom. What were the results?

---

11. How can you responsibly use your power of influence to strengthen the men in your life?

12. How can you test yourself to be sure your perspective comes from God and that your thinking is not skewed by the Enemy?

13. Have you ever forgotten the heartbeat or purpose behind the relationships God has given you? What was the result?

14. What can you do to gain, revive or strengthen a sense of purpose for your life? Through this can you gain a measure of restoration for your lost paradise? Why or why not?

_____

_____

_____

_____

_____

_____

_____

_____

_____

_____

15. Are you tapping into your powers of insight and influence to heal and nurture? How so or why not? How could you do this better? What do you think the result would be?

_____

_____

_____

_____

_____

_____

_____

_____

_____

_____

> **The Lord announces victory, and throngs of women shout the happy news. Enemy kings and their armies flee, while the women of Israel divide the plunder.**
> Psalm 68:11-12 NLT

Make It Yours

Are you ready to face your fears and become part of the joyous throng? What areas of loss are you ready to declare victory over?

Notes

What If I Don't Like Women? 2

Read chapter 2 of *Fight Like a Girl* and view DVD session 2.

What could possibly cause a large portion of the female populace to reject their own gender?

Insight

The truth is now I love women, although there was a time when I was not particularly fond of women. Not only did I not like women, I resented being one. Therefore I was not surprised by the concert of anti-female sentiment from my fellow sisters. I have heard one form or another of this sentiment expressed by women of all ages and walks of life.

1. Do you dislike women? Do you resent being one? Why? Press yourself to determine whether your reasons are based on truth or stereotypes.

_____

_____

_____

_____

_____

_____

_____

_____

2. Does your approach to life tend to be more masculine or more feminine? Do you take pride or feel shame in either approach? Where do you think those feelings come from? Do you wish you could be more one and less the other?

_____

_____

_____

_____

_____

_____

3. How do you feel when you are with other women who articulate their general disgust with females? Does this create in you a sense of connection or discomfort? Why?

_____

_____

_____

_____

_____

_____

_____

4. What emotions generally underlie a woman's dislike for other women—jealousy? fear? anger? annoyance? Has disliking other women ever alleviated any of these feelings for you? Has it ever solved the underlying emotions? Why or why not?

_____

_____

_____

_____

_____

5. What does being a woman mean to you? Where did you learn this attitude?

_____

_____

_____

_____

_____

_____

_____

_____

_____

_____

_____

_____

_____

BIG *Idea*

This lack of aware-ness of feminine value needs to be confronted in almost every realm of life if we are to see a turnaround. God is awakening our individuality so we can realize what we can become as daugh-ters, wives, mothers, sisters, lead-ers, and friends. Women have sig-nificant contributions to make to their unique spheres of influence, and these will never fully be real-ized with an underlying distaste for our gender. (p. 13)

6. What are some of the roles you play as a woman? What is inspiring about those roles and what contributions have you made because of them?

_____

_____

_____

_____

_____

_____

7. What perception does society have of women today? How is it similar to or different from God's view of women? Explain.

_____

_____

_____

_____

_____

8. Has being a woman worked to your advantage or disadvantage? Describe specific situations where your gender has affected how others treated you.

_____

_____

_____

_____

_____

_____

_____

9. What do you do when you are treated poorly—or when you see others being treated poorly—because of gender?

_____

_____

_____

_____

_____

_____

_____

_____

ACTIVITY
You Are to Be Applauded
Leader: Choose an adjective that describes women and apply that word to someone in the room (e.g., "Helen is beautiful.").

Go around the circle, letting each woman (including Helen) offer a synonym for that word (e.g., gorgeous, lovely, pretty, stunning). If someone cannot think of a new word within two seconds, she is "out"—and the game continues. The winner is the woman who stays in the game the longest.

Where there is no vision, the people perish.
Proverbs 29:18 KJV

10. Can you recall a specific time when you were especially glad to be a woman? Describe the circumstances that triggered this response.

_____

_____

_____

_____

_____

_____

_____

_____

_____

_____

_____

_____

BIG *Idea*

I am looking for something more. I long for the day when daughters will begin to weave this garment and restore the unique splendor, love, and beauty that only the expression of the feminine brings. I am watching for women who know how to adorn not only their lives but also the lives of others with a portion of heaven's splendor. (p. 17)

BIG *Idea*

In order to find our way, we must first turn off the ever-present static, because it dangerously muffles and distorts all we hear. This interference had become a constant in my life. I even heard its persistent distortion as I read the Scriptures. I heard it in marriage relational dynamics. I heard it in sitcoms. I heard it in policies and procedures. I heard it in humor. I heard it in church. I heard it in school. What did the static say? "Women are a problem." (p. 18)

11. How has God revealed that women are significant?

_____

_____

_____

_____

_____

_____

_____

_____

_____

_____

_____

_____

12. Have you heard the static of the lie that states "Women are a problem"? When did you first hear it? In which areas of life have you heard it?

_____

_____

_____

_____

_____

_____

It is not good for the man to be alone.
I will make a companion who will help him.
Genesis 2:18 NLT

13. Because truth displaces lies, how did you feel when you heard you are an *answer* not a *problem*? And even more than this, how did you feel when you heard that you are *God's answer*?

_____

_____

_____

_____

_____

_____

BIG *Idea*

You are a vital part of God's answer for humanity. Our heavenly Father has specifically formed you to do a task no other woman can accomplish in our space and time. God says, "I like women. They are an answer to so many problems." (p. 22)

14. With this paradigm shift, how will your approach to other women and your own feminine self-image change?

_____

_____

_____

_____

_____

_____

_____

15. In which areas of life where you may have formerly thought yourself a problem might you actually be an answer? Which of your gifts are latent, just waiting to be used? State one action you will take today to live out this truth.

_____

_____

_____

_____

_____

_____

_____

16. Do you know someone who sees herself as a problem? What can you do to encourage her to recover her value as a woman of God?

_____

_____

_____

_____

_____

_____

_____

_____

BIG *Idea*

Think of it! You are somebody's answer. You are something's answer. There is a problem out there only your presence can solve. There is a broken and wounded heart to which only you can administer healing. You are a voice to the mute. You are beauty amid desolation. (p. 19)

Let me see your face, let me hear your voice; for your voice is sweet, and your face is lovely.
Song of Solomon 2:14 NKJV

There is a world that longs to see and hear you. The daughters of Eve have foolishly believed a lie and allowed it to change their perspective and image. By embracing the lie that we were a problem, as time passed we became one. (p. 20)

Make It Yours

Have you ever participated in negative self-talk ("I hate that I'm a girl.... I wish I were a guy!") about your gender? In light of the truth, do you now see it as a lie? Rewrite the dialogue about your femininity.

_____

_____

_____

_____

_____

_____

_____

_____

_____

_____

_____

_____

_____

_____

_____

_____

_____

_____

_____

_____

_____

_____

_____

_____

_____

But I Am Not a Man

Read chapter 3 of *Fight Like a Girl* and view DVD session 3.

3

Men and women have wrestled each other for far too long, and the time of awakening is at hand. We are not enemies…we are beloved allies.

Insight

As time passes, gender dynamics will become increasingly key and important. I have heard gender discrimination cited as the last prejudice to be addressed, but I feel we err to describe gender as an issue of prejudice. It is an issue of life and death.

LOCATE YOURSELF

Am I an Imposter?

1. I feel vulnerable when I cry in public.
   True or False

2. I often discount my gut reaction and make a calculated analysis.
   True or False

3. I see men as strong and women as weak.
   True or False

4. I have few female role models.
   True or False

5. I would rather be called a tomboy than a lady.
   True or False

SCORE

If you chose True more than False, you are likely more false than true. Take some time to get in touch with your feminine side.

If you chose False more than True, you are woman and proud of it. Use your femininity wisely.

---

1. How significant is the gender issue to you? How have you seen gender discrimination played out in your life or in society?

_____

_____

_____

_____

_____

_____

_____

_____

2. Do you think there is a difference between gender discrimination and other prejudices? Why or why not?

_____

_____

_____

_____

_____

_____

_____

3. What would it look like if men and women were to unite and see each other as allies on every level?

_____

_____

_____

_____

_____

_____

_____

_____

_____

_____

BIG *Idea*

For years, our culture has tried to minimize or even deny the existence of gender and the power it exerts on so many facets of life. Could this be why we have lost so much of our former strength and core bearing? Is this the kink that has left our nations, cultures, churches, families, children, and marriages with a distinct and serious wobble? (p. 25)

4. Why do you think people want to ignore or minimize the existence of gender differences? How do you see this happening?

_____

_____

_____

_____

_____

_____

5. Do you think our culture is weakened by its refusal to acknowledge the differences between men and women? Explain your answer in regard to our churches, our marriages, and our children.

_____

_____

_____

_____

_____

_____

6. What evidence is there that men and women the world over are desperate for wholeness? Is this true for you personally? Explain your answer.

_____

_____

_____

_____

_____

_____

_____

_____

7. What are some of the inherent differences between men and women? Do you think the differences between men and women are taught or inherited? Back up your answer with examples.

_____

_____

_____

_____

_____

_____

_____

_____

8. Imagine what the world would be like if the only difference between men and women were their body structure. Would androgyny bring true freedom to either gender? Why or why not?

_____

_____

_____

_____

_____

_____

_____

9. How do you think Adam felt when he first beheld Eve? Why was she the perfect partner for him? How would you feel if a man received you with such delight? (p. 26)

_____

_____

_____

_____

_____

_____

10. What strengths do you have that complement the men in your life?

_____

_____

_____

_____

_____

_____

_____

_____

_____

_____

_____

_____

BIG *Idea*

Women, understand it was not a man but a serpent that trespassed on our lives and robbed us. By way of cunning and deception he stripped us of our beauty, dominion, and power. With the fall, our vision was darkened. In the dark, it is easy to mistake enemies for friends and friends for enemies. In the realm of shadow, we often perceive differences as threats. Men and women have wrestled each other for far too long, and the time of awakening is at hand. We are not enemies . . . we are beloved allies. (p. 27)

11. Do you sometimes think of men as your enemy? If so, what factors contributed to this attitude? If not, what contributed to your healthy view of men?

_____

_____

_____

_____

_____

12. Have you felt societal pressure to harden yourself, to become tougher? How have you responded to this pressure?

BIG *Idea*

Confused by past issues of pain, our culture has encouraged men to get in touch with their feminine side. While this is happening, women are coached to be more aggressive and masculine in their approach to life. Men are repeatedly asked to be *more* vulnerable or defenseless, while women have been persuaded to harden themselves. (p. 27)

_____

_____

_____

_____

_____

_____

_____

_____

_____

_____

_____

_____

_____

13. Do you see the men in your life as strong protectors? Why or why not?

_____

_____

_____

_____

_____

_____

_____

_____

_____

_____

_____

_____

_____

14. Do you feel as if you are sometimes in a game with men as opponents? If so, should striving to be "fair and even" be the ultimate goal? Why or why not?

15. Why is it important to be uniquely powerful as a male or female?

How does this fit with the following admonition of the Holy Spirit?

For you truly are not a man, and there are yet battles in the spirit for the sons to fight, and there are yet battles in the spirit for the daughters to fight. Begin to call forth the daughters; cry out for them now. Call the daughters to wage the wars only they can win, and to fight the battles as only my daughters can, because truly the enemy fears this revelation more than he fears any woman who fights like a man. (p. 34)

16. In what areas of life have you slipped onto the battlefield disguised as a man? Why did you take on this façade? What was the result? Why do you think women are afraid to reveal themselves?

_____

_____

_____

_____

_____

_____

_____

_____

_____

_____

17. Why do you think the Enemy wants us to try to become something we're not?

_____

_____

_____

_____

_____

_____

_____

_____

_____

_____

**Some women, through faith, received their
loved ones back again from death.**
Hebrews 11:35 TLB

Make It Yours

Women have the power to turn what looks like death into life. Record ways you can strip off the masculine disguise in your life.

_____

_____

_____

_____

_____

_____

_____

_____

_____

_____

_____

_____

_____

_____

_____

_____

_____

_____

_____

_____

_____

_____

_____

_____

_____

_____

_____

_____

Notes

Finding Center

Read chapter 4 of *Fight Like a Girl* and view DVD session 3.

4

By standing firm you will gain life.
–Luke 21:19 NIV

Insight

Finding center is not the same as being mediocre. Finding center is a place of balance and a place of strength. It is where perspective is restored and truth recovered. Center is the safe base of an absolute in a world of upheaval. It is a connection with the God constant.

LOCATE YOURSELF

Am I Centered?

1. I read magazines or the newspaper more than I read the Bible.
   True or False

2. I believe the Bible is subjective truth.
   True or False

3. I am more comfortable in the presence of people than in the presence of God.
   True or False

4. I believe gender is environmentally influenced.
   True or False

1. After reviewing the big idea, in what areas of life do you personally see this collapse?

   _____

   _____

   _____

   _____

   _____

   _____

   _____

   _____

   _____

   _____

   _____

   _____

   _____

BIG *Idea*

Nature itself rebels against our presumption and arrogance. For far too long we've made choices that only served the immediate and forgot legacy. I sense a slow and steady collapse. Families are fragmented, nations are divided, government and financial institutions are crumbling. Creation is not well. Its guardians and keepers have left their posts. If our reckless choices have brought destruction, doesn't it stand to reason we can be part of the restoration? There is only one hope of light coming from this darkness. People must choose to live for something more than the immediate. (pp. 36-37)

2. Do you see hope for restoration? Why or why not? What can we do to improve the situation?

   _____

   _____

   _____

   _____

   _____

   _____

3. What have we sacrificed in our quest for a less unique way of life?

_____

_____

_____

_____

_____

_____

_____

_____

_____

_____

_____

_____

_____

_____

_____

_____

_____

BIG *Idea*

This world has contracted and shrunk proportionally as the multiple levels of communication technology have expanded. The globe is networked as the cords that once hung so loosely between cultures and nations are intertwined and tightened. There have never been so many voices speaking at once. There is so much noise and yet so little clarity. While we are advancing on many fronts, much ground has been lost on others. As the world accelerates, its very core has become unstable. There is no safe base. No place of peace and quiet where all activity stops. (p. 37)

4. Where is your place of peace, quiet and safety?

_____

_____

_____

_____

_____

_____

_____

BIG *Idea*

The human soul is sick and lonely. We've been entertained for so long by the unreal and untrue, nothing truly real moves us. Atrocities no longer break our hearts as long as we are safe. We may get angry, but then it fades. Children are growing up in atmospheres so hardened they have no capacity for remorse or regret. Individuals exist without purpose and direction because there is nothing greater in their lives than themselves. There is no compass pointing to true North. Truth is relative as we walk in circles, unable to find our center. (p. 38)

5. Can hearts be hardened and lonely at the same time? Explain your answer. How does the state of our heart affect others?

_____

_____

_____

_____

_____

_____

_____

_____

_____

_____

_____

_____

_____

6. Do you feel as though you are heading in the right direction? How can we be sure we're walking in truth? Explain your answer.

_____

_____

_____

_____

_____

_____

_____

_____

_____

_____

> **Claiming to be wise, they became utter fools instead.**
> Romans 1:22 NLT

7. How can we become fools? In what ways are you seeing this happen?

    _____

    _____

    _____

    _____

    _____

    _____

8. Is our culture currently moving toward light or darkness? What evidence do you have for your answer?

    _____

    _____

    _____

    _____

    _____

9. Why do you think Satan wants us to act like men? What's in it for him, and how does his plan hurt us?

    _____

    _____

    _____

    _____

    _____

    _____

BIG *Idea*

Our Enemy fears the revelation of God's daughters more than he fears women who act like men. Why would he be afraid of women who behave like men any more than he would fear men who act like women? When men and women are not true to their cores, both genders are out of sync and removed from their positions of strength. Neither guise frightens him, for he has worked long and hard to confound the strengths and magnify the weaknesses of both sexes. (p. 40)

10. Why are Satan's half-truths more effective in deceiving us than full-blown lies? What are some of these half-truths?

_____

_____

_____

_____

_____

_____

_____

_____

11. In what areas have we exchanged the truth for a lie? (p. 40)

_____

_____

_____

_____

_____

_____

_____

_____

**The path of the righteous is like the first gleam of dawn,
shining ever brighter till the full light of day.**
Proverbs 4:18

12. Define *male* and *female*. (p. 41)

_____

_____

_____

_____

_____

13. What qualifies or disqualifies a leader?

_____

_____

_____

_____

_____

_____

_____

> **From him the whole body, joined and held together by every**
> **supporting ligament, grows and builds itself up in love,**
> **as each part does its work.**
> Ephesians 4:16 NIV

BIG *Idea*

The verse does not say "as the women do the men's part" or "as the men do the women's part," then we will be built up. It very clearly says each part must do its work if the whole is to function properly. (p. 44)

14. In reference to women as connectors, what happens when we neglect wounded women in the church? (pp. 44-45)

_____

_____

_____

_____

_____

_____   .

_____

_____

_____

_____

_____

_____

> **He has made us competent as ministers of a new covenant-not of the letter**
> **but of the Spirit; for the letter kills, but the Spirit gives life.**
> 2 Corinthians 3:6 NIV

15. Who makes us competent to minister? Is it an organization, license, or ordination?

_____

_____

_____

_____

16. Have you ever thought, "Because I am not a man, I have no valid contribution"? If so, how has this attitude affected your relationships, activities, or self-image?

_____

_____

_____

_____

And if the ear should say, "Because I am not an eye, I do not belong to the body,"it would not for that reason cease to be part of the body. If the whole body were an eye, where would the sense of hearing be? If the whole body were an ear, where would the sense of smell be? But in fact God has arranged the parts in the body, every one of them, just as he wanted them to be.

1 Corinthians 12:16-18 NIV

17. In what ways can women function in their strengths in the house of God?

BIG *Idea*

The answer has never been for the woman to have no part, just as it is not for the woman to have the man's part; but rather, the woman is to have her own part. (p. 46) There is an amazing combination found when you marry strength with beauty, authority with wisdom, male with female. It was always God's idea....two with one heart. Together, we realize a multiplication of our strengths. (p. 49)

_____

_____

_____

Make It Yours

Write some ways you will enhance your part in the body of Christ.

Notes

Who's the Man?

Read chapter 5 of *Fight Like a Girl* and view DVD session 4.

5

**I am careful not to confuse excellence with perfection.
Excellence, I can reach for; perfection is God's business.
–Michael J. Fox**

Insight

Jesus loved women and allowed them intimate contact in uncomfortable situations. Whether speaking to a woman shunned by others as she drew water from the well or allowing Himself to be anointed in the midst of judgment, He never pulled away. When Mary sat at His feet, He would not allow the busy Martha to remove her. He is the only man who will never disappoint you.

---

1. How has Jesus proven Himself to be "the Man" in your life?

_____

_____

_____

_____

_____

_____

_____

_____

2. Do you believe Jesus—who is the Son of Man and the Son of God—loves women and values them deeply? Why or why not?

_____

_____

_____

_____

_____

_____

_____

3. Since so many women have experienced betrayal, disappointment, or rejection by a man, do you think it is wise for us to look to a masculine God to supply our needs? Why or why not? How does He prove we can trust Him?

_____

_____

_____

_____

_____

_____

_____

_____

God is not a man, that he should lie, nor a son of man, that he should change his mind. Does he speak and then not act? Does he promise and not fulfill?
Numbers 23:19 NIV

4. In what ways does our culture still see other people as the answer to our problems?

_____

_____

_____

Worldview: "The perfect man = the perfect life" (p. 54)

5. In what ways have you looked to men or other women to be something only God can be to you?

6. How do some magazines or books displace the truth of God? Give an example.

BIG *Idea*

With high hopes of perfection and happiness, most women marry the man of their dreams and watch the dream slowly morph into a nightmare! Desperate to keep the dream alive, they attempt to train the man, radically change the man, and if these methods don't work, they just decide to be the man! (p. 54)

7. If applicable, in what ways have you tried to change your husband?

_____

_____

_____

_____

_____

_____

_____

_____

_____

_____

_____

_____

_____

8. Do you know anyone who believes that winning the perfect man will grant her the perfect life? What do you think created this kind of thinking?

_____

_____

_____

_____

_____

_____

9. What happens when a woman attempts to train a man to fit her image of perfection? What are the pressures on the man? What are the pressures on the woman?

_____

_____

_____

_____

_____

_____

10. When a woman fails in her attempt to train the man to fit her image of perfection, what happens to the relationship? What happens to the man? What happens to the woman?

_____

_____

_____

_____

_____

_____

_____

11. Who is the ultimate keeper of promises? Who remembers them all?

_____

_____

_____

_____

_____

BIG *Idea*

It should be a relief to all of us, male and female alike, that God is not like us. God is God, and there is no one like Him. Only He is the faithful and true witness. His perspective is not skewed or obscured by this earthly realm. He cannot be bribed or deceived. (p. 56)

12. Do you think people accept the fact that God is not like us? Or do they expect from Him the same failings they expect from people?

_____

_____

_____

_____

_____

_____

_____

_____

BIG *Idea*

Another way we elevate man to the god-level is when we mistakenly believe people are the source of security and promotion. This could happen when we expect friends to meet all our emotional and supportive needs. Further, the mind-set of the "god-man" has infiltrated the business world, where many mistakenly believe networking and name-dropping are the quickest route to favor, promotion, or provision. Those hungry for the approval of man will become users. (p. 56)

13. Do you struggle with relying on people as your source? If so, confess the areas where you have sought promotion outside of God.

_____

_____

_____

_____

_____

_____

_____

_____

_____

_____

_____

_____

14. Have you ever been disappointed when a person failed to provide the security you expected from him or her? Explain your answer.

_____

_____

_____

_____

_____

_____

_____

_____

_____

BIG *Idea*

Favor with people is all about who we are in public. Everything hinges on the public's perception of us. This is usually forged by appearance and achievement. In this arena, the attractive and successful consistently win. When their popularity wavers, they will suffer loss if they tie their worth to people's opinions. (p. 57)

15. Give an example of someone who was popular last year and out of favor this year (a celebrity perhaps).

_____

_____

_____

_____

16. Name someone who does not seem to waver with popular opinion.

_____

_____

_____

_____

_____

17. Have you ever enjoyed public favor only to lose it? How did God respond to you in that season?

_____

_____

_____

_____

BIG *Idea*

God does not waver in His love toward us, no matter what the public's opinion of us may be. Favor with God is realized in secret. It focuses on who we are in private when no one is around to applaud or cheer. Who we are "off the record" is a much more accurate representation of who we truly are. (p. 57)

18. Have you spent enough time with God in private so He can reveal who you are in Him? If so, what has He made clear to you?

_____

_____

_____

_____

_____

_____

_____

19. Do you behave differently when no one is watching? Where are the most crucial decisions made—in public or in private?

_____

_____

_____

_____

_____

_____

_____

_____

20. Who do you fear disappointing more—people or God? What consequences have you faced when you've disappointed people?

_____

_____

_____

_____

_____

_____

_____

**Fear of man will prove to be a snare,
but whoever trusts in the LORD is kept safe.**
Proverbs 29:25 NIV

21. As God is exalted, our life posture will change. List the areas you need to declare God as more than enough for you.

_____

_____

_____

_____

**They exchanged the truth of
God for a lie, and worshiped
and served created things
rather than the Creator–who
is forever praised. Amen.**
Romans 1:25 NIV

BIG *Idea*

Far too often, frail humans exchange the truth for the lie, substance for shadow, life for death. If we have in any way exchanged the truth for a lie, then we can in fact decide to exchange our lies for His truth. It all begins with telling God the Father He is Truth; He is our source of worth and more than enough for us.

In God I trust; I will not be afraid. What can man do to me?
Psalm 56:11 NIV

Make It Yours

Do you need to exchange a lie for God's truth? Write your lies along with His truth and make the exchange.

_____

_____

_____

_____

_____

_____

_____

_____

_____

_____

_____

_____

_____

_____

_____

_____

_____

_____

_____

_____

_____

_____

_____

_____

_____

_____

_____

_____

_____

_____

_____

"While reading Fight Like A Girl God took me back through my past and then said, 'Girl, these were firecrackers fired at you. Now, in your hands they have become weapons of Satan's demise.'"

When Do Women Strike?

Read chapter 6 of *Fight Like a Girl* and view DVD session 5.

Never yield to the apparently overwhelming might of the enemy.
–Winston Churchill

> *Insight*
>
> Women strike when the Enemy draws near. Whenever Satan trespasses the boundaries of love and life and comes within range, it is not us, but he, who should tremble. For when we find ourselves ensnared in unavoidable conflict, God will strengthen us to fight with whatever is in our hands.

LOCATE YOURSELF

What is My Fighting Style?

1. I'm at a social gathering, and a woman is defending the actions of someone I see as brutal. My response is to:
   A. tell her she's wrong and that she needs to rethink her position.
   B. seek out the pain she must have in her heart so I can comfort her.
   C. engage her in a thoughtful debate.
   D. keep silent, assuming others will recognize the error of her ways.
   E. interrupt, making sure she isn't given an opportunity to speak on the topic any further.

2. I'm held hostage by a bank robber. My response is to
   A. insist that he is making a big mistake and beg him to let me go.
   B. lead him to Christ.
   C. explain why his plan will not work.
   D. wait for the right moment to escape.
   E. grab his weapon and deliver him to the police.

3. My neighbor's house is on fire and there is a child inside. My response is to
   A. dash into the house to get the child.
   B. take care of the needs of my neighbor during this stressful time.
   C. devise an effective plan for rescuing the child.
   D. clear people away from the house as I wait for the rescue team.
   E. try to put out the fire.

SCORE

If you chose mostly As, you fight by *confronting.* Your purpose is to fix the problem.
If you chose mostly Bs, you fight by *loving.* Your purpose is to help the person
   with the problem.
If you chose mostly Cs, you fight by *arguing.* Your purpose is to resist the enemy.
If you chose mostly Ds, you fight by *resisting.* Your purpose is to trust God.
If you chose mostly Es, you fight by *attacking.* Your purpose is to destroy
   the enemy.

---

1. Review the biblical examples of women who have struck out when the enemy drew
   near. As far as you can tell, was their timing right? Why or why not? (p. 64)

   _____

   _____

   _____

   _____

   _____

   _____

   _____

   _____

   _____

2. Do you believe women were designed to seek out physical conflict on a literal battle field with men, or should it be a last resort? Why or why not?

---

3. Our reasons behind confrontation need to be motivated by what preserves life, honor, truth, and virtue. Give some examples of what this might look like.

BIG *Idea*

Both genders should choose battles wisely. If we find conflict in our way that has come to destroy what we guard, then we have no choice but to fight with whatever means we find available. When evil presents itself and blocks our paths, there is no other recourse for the daughters of Eve. We were formed to do all within our power to prevent death and loss, as well as to promote the dignity and preservation of life and virtue. In these pursuits, we must never foolishly draw back in fear. (pp. 64-65)

---

4. Do you look for conflict?

_____

_____

_____

_____

_____

_____

_____

_____

_____

5. According to Genesis 3:15, what do women fight with?

BIG *Idea*

Women intimately partner with God as they bear and raise children. They are our seed and His heritage and reward. They are the ones we launch into the future. They live far beyond us with eyes that see up close what we see only far off. Their ears will hear out loud things that were only sounded as a whisper in our lifetimes. They are to be carefully aimed and propelled, for they will not easily miss their marks. We are promised, by raising them in the way they should go, they will be more inclined to hit the target of their destiny in God when they are grown. (p. 66)

To answer the following questions, first review the excerpt on page 65 from C. S. Lewis's *The Lion, The Witch and the Wardrobe*.

6. Susan was entrusted with arrows. Did you know your children were likened to this form of weaponry?

_____

_____

_____

_____

_____

_____

_____

7. The second gift of Susan's was a horn that guaranteed help. Why is our gift of prayer even more certain?

_____

_____

_____

BIG *Idea*

In order to approach God in faith when we pray, we need to remember two major points: First, God is always the bigger, better answer; second, we need to trust that He has already made a way. In prayer then, we should confidently sound the horn when we see danger looming.

Before they call I will answer; while they are still speaking I will hear.
Isaiah 65:24 NIV

8. When does God answer our prayers?

_____

_____

_____

_____

_____

_____

_____

_____

9. How frequently has God answered your prayers in the manner and time frame you desired?

_____

_____

_____

_____

BIG *Idea*

We will draw back when we forget the gifts God has promised us as His daughters, and we remain silent when our voices should be raised. We foolishly compare our gifts with the gifts of others, and deem ours weak or inferior by comparison. At other times, we look at the futility of our situations and imagine God's ability is not sufficient to tackle the messes we've made. Know this: there is a battle, the damage is extensive, and it is no longer about us. (p. 67)

**Call to Me, and I will answer you, and show you great
and mighty things, which you do not know.**
Jeremiah 33:3 NKJV

10. "Why not the gift of a sword and shield?" Did you see yourself in Lucy's question? How have women been weakened by comparing their gifts with the gifts given to men?

_____

_____

_____

_____

_____

_____

_____

_____

11. Do you fear you will be denied a chance to prove your love?

_____

_____

_____

_____

_____

_____

_____

_____

12. Do you feel resentful when you can't express your devotion to God in the way that men can? If not, why not? If so, what do you do about it? What should you do about it?

_____

_____

_____

_____

_____

_____

_____

13. Do you truly understand our differences are for strength?

_____

_____

_____

_____

_____

_____

_____

_____

_____

_____

_____

BIG *Idea*

I think God always intended us for a higher purpose than a warrior of blood-shed.... He formed women as warriors for life. There are many ways to wage battles without bloodshed.

Tell me, is it nobler to stretch forth your hand to strike and wound, or to administer healing? What is more valuable, taking life or elevating it? Is there more power to be found in laying siege to a city or in feeding an enemy?

_____

_____

_____

_____

_____

A gentle answer turns away wrath, but a harsh word stirs up anger.
Proverbs 15:1 NIV

14. How have you seen the above verse played out in your life? Have you ever been sorry for answering gently?

_____

_____

_____

_____

_____

_____

_____

15. Like Joan of Arc, how can you hold up the standard during the battles of life and lift the eyes of others heavenward?

16. What do you think about the description of women as an unsuspected weapon? (pp. 73-74)

17. How often do you doubt the value of your contribution? Do you believe you have been entrusted with a treasure? Do you believe you have what you need to make it in life?

She...provides food for her household,... She extends her hands to the poor, yes, she reaches out her hands to the needy. She is not afraid of snow for her household, for all her household is clothed with scarlet.
Proverbs 31:15, 20-21 NKJV

18. Have you ever sought God through prayer and fasting before confronting an issue? What area of conflict now threatens your life and family? Rather than responding in fear, can you believe you were divinely positioned to fight?

_____

_____

_____

_____

_____

_____

_____

_____

_____

_____

_____

_____

_____

_____

_____

_____

If you keep quiet at a time like this, deliverance for the Jews will arise from some other place, but you and your relatives will die. What's more, who can say but that you have been elevated to the palace for just such a time as this?
Esther 4:14 NLT

BIG *Idea*

We will never truly recover our power or purpose if our vision is limited. Healthy families and individuals reach out. We can become so entangled with our own family dynamics that our world shrinks and contracts on itself. The virtuous woman of Proverbs 31 had a healthy understanding of reaching out.

She is unafraid that by extending her hand her household will suffer loss. We also see the dynamics of how to fight in the life of Queen Esther....Esther was a weapon of divine precision strategically hidden away in a palace. Though a queen, Esther realized something most have forgotten: None of us are isolated. If we imagine ourselves untouchable or think our fortresses impenetrable, we will soon see them fall....Esther sounded the alarm and released her arrows. (pp. 74-76)

Make It Yours

Daughter, you are both strategic and valuable. You are the insight to recognize the Enemy's approach. You are the intuition to hear what is really being said in his threats. You are the agent of healing. You are the unsuspected one he will learn to fear. You are the missing piece we all need.

Write the specific prayers you need God to answer.

_____

_____

_____

_____

_____

_____

_____

_____

_____

_____

_____

_____

_____

_____

_____

_____

_____

_____

_____

_____

_____

_____

_____

Notes

Fighting with Wisdom

7

Read chapter 7 of *Fight Like a Girl* and view DVD session 6.

God gives wisdom, knowledge, and joy to those who please him.
–Ecclesiastes 2:26 NLT

Insight

God repeatedly invites us to ask Him for wisdom. He wants to impart wisdom even more than we want to attain it. Part of fighting like a girl is recovering everything that was the woman's to steward. Wisdom is portrayed in the first nine chapters of Proverbs in the female pronoun. It is time that the daughters of God be known for their wisdom in every situation.

LOCATE YOURSELF

Am I Wise?

(1=I've rarely said/thought this; 5=I've often said/thought this)

1. Wisdom is a function of education.
     1 2 3 4 5

2. Wisdom is the result of experience.
     1 2 3 4 5

3. Wisdom is inherited from others.
     1 2 3 4 5

4. Wisdom is available to a predetermined few.
    1 2 3 4 5

5. Wisdom is androgynous, having neither male nor female characteristics.
    1 2 3 4 5

SCORE
5-10: You call wisdom your sister and seek after her with a pure heart.
11-18: You are in a great position for growth. Begin calling wisdom your sister.
19-25: You will gain much from this chapter. Continue to dig deeper by reading a chapter of Proverbs a day.

GO DEEPER

Some of you may have imagined wisdom to be a function of experience. Yet we all know people who seem to go through the same thing over and over again without ever becoming any wiser. Wisdom is available to anyone who will pursue her. This means no matter your age, gender, education, birth right, or life experiences, wisdom can be captured and realized in your life.

1. In your group discuss some attributes of sisters and how wisdom can play that role (e.g., confidante, friend, advocate, and so forth).

_____

_____

_____

_____

_____

_____

_____

_____

_____

_____

BIG *Idea*

In *Fight Like a Girl* wisdom was defined as "the intimate embrace of truth." Because wisdom is portrayed in relational imagery in the Bible, I believe it can become our counselor and friend.

Wisdom has the power to transform those who apprehend it...when truth merges with our being and begins to drive and direct our actions, everything changes. Proverbs 7:4 admonishes us to call wisdom our sister. (pp. 80-81)

2. Looking at our culture's presentation of women, do you think we women have lost our intimate portrayal of wisdom because we were negligent, or did we willfully choose to listen to the counsel of foolishness? Explain your answer.

_____

_____

_____

_____

_____

_____

_____

_____

3. As daughters, how can we recover our name of wisdom?

_____

_____

_____

_____

_____

_____

_____

_____

4. *Fight Like a Girl* cited the major difference between wise women and foolish women as knowing when to let go and when to hold on. Do you agree or disagree? Why?

_____

_____

_____

_____

_____

_____

5. Because wisdom is a dynamic of exchange, list some areas that you are presently holding on to that you need to let go of. List some areas that you have let go of that you need to recapture.

LET GO OF   LAY HOLD OF

_____   _____
_____   _____
_____   _____
_____   _____
_____   _____
_____   _____
_____   _____

6. Why do you think the author of Proverbs depicts both wisdom and foolishness as female?

_____
_____
_____
_____
_____
_____

It is interesting that so many attributes that describe women also capture our desire for wisdom. Example: women give life, wisdom gives life; women give legacy, wisdom gives legacy; women are desirable, wisdom is desirable.

7. What area in our culture do you think is most desperate for wisdom?

_____
_____
_____
_____
_____

8. Do you find the concept of wisdom intimidating? Why or why not?

_____

_____

_____

_____

_____

_____

_____

_____

_____

_____

_____

_____

_____

BIG *Idea*

Wisdom in Relationships: There is nothing more frustrating than feeling responsible for something you have no ability to change. We are not responsible for how people respond to us, but only for our actions toward them. Often women have a really hard time knowing when to let go of a relationship that has gotten unhealthy or when to break free from unhealthy patterns within relationships. It is time that we allow wisdom to dictate our friendships and how we interact with each other so that we will truly be answers and not problems.

Understand that God knew wisdom would be intimidating in our eyes, and that is why He asked us to exchange our ways for his ways.

9. How do you feel about the following commentary? Discuss the following guidelines in relational dynamics:

As godly wise women we need to understand that we can only go so far to effect change in relationships. If nothing happens, we have no choice but to let it go and entrust it into the hands of God. This means we bless and move on. We exchange frustration for release. We release what is in our hands so God can release what is in His. (p. 82.)

_____

_____

_____

_____

10. Is there a relationship you need to bless, release, and move on from? Right now, compose a blessing for that person to communicate later.

_____

_____

_____

_____

_____

_____

_____

_____

_____

_____

It is never easy to let go of things we cannot change. This is why the Bible includes so many stories of women who exemplified this dynamic of exchange. Reviewing the chapter, which stories spoke to you the most and why? (Pick at least two.) Below is a brief synopsis from the book:

Eve exchanged death for the hope of redemption.

Sarah exchanged fear for faith.

Tamar exchanged widowhood for motherhood, and treachery for honor.

Rahab exchanged fear of judgment for fear of the Lord.

Naomi and Ruth exchanged grief and loss for adoption and legacy.

Hannah exchanged dishonor for honor, offense for victory, and barrenness for a lineage of prophets.

Abigail exchanged the foolishness of her husband for the life of her household and counseled a king when her own husband wouldn't listen.

Jael exchanged ungodly alliances for godly ones.

Bathsheba exchanged scandal and death for honor, wisdom, legacy, and promise.

Elizabeth exchanged years of disappointment for God's promise.

Mary exchanged uncertainty and shame for the surety of God's promise and favor.

The fear of the Lord is the beginning of wisdom; all who follow
his precepts have good understanding.
Psalm 111:10 NIV

_____

_____

_____

_____

_____

_____

_____

_____

11. Looking back over your life, describe two or three opportunities you had to listen to either the counsel of fear or of wisdom. Has fear ever been a good counselor?

_____

_____

_____

_____

_____

_____

Come, my children, listen to me;
I will teach you the fear of the Lord.
Whoever of you loves life and desires
to see many good days, keep your tongue
from evil and your lips from speaking
lies. Turn from evil and do good;
seek peace and pursue it.
Psalm 34:11-14 NIV

BIG *Idea*

All these women are not really different from us. Each day presented them with choices just as this day presents us with choices. We must determine to deliberately choose wisdom, or we will find ourselves walking in foolishness by default. Wisdom is tied to our fear of the Lord. The fear of the Lord is almost an alien concept in most of the church culture, yet Proverbs calls it the beginning of wisdom. If we are going to be wise, we need to embrace the fear of the Lord.

12. What might the life of somebody who fears the Lord look like? Remember it is tied to wisdom and beauty, riches and honor.

_____

_____

_____

_____

_____

_____

_____

_____

13. Because wisdom is intimately tied to our fear of the Lord, and understanding is related to our response to evil, it is important to understand what God loves and what He hates. Scripture tells us God hates foolishness and evil and loves wisdom and justice. Make a list of some things you would say God loves and hates in your life. Make a list of some things you would say God loves and hates in our culture.

_____

_____

_____

_____

_____

_____

_____

_____

_____

_____

_____

_____

BIG *Idea*

Because our heavenly Father stores up wisdom, waiting to give it freely without prejudice or partiality, we have only to ask Him. He promises to accept what we bring Him in exchange. We present our foolishness and lack of answers, and He in return gives us His wisdom, direction, and counsel. (p. 92)

Make It Yours

Proverbs is divided into 31 chapters. Take five minutes each day to read one chapter. You will be amazed at what you glean.

> Happy is the person who finds wisdom and gains understanding.
> For the profit of wisdom is better than silver, and her wages are
> better than gold. Wisdom is more precious that rubies; nothing you
> desire can compare with her. She offers you life in her right hand, and
> riches and honor in her left. She will guide you down delightful paths;
> all her ways are satisfying. Wisdom is a tree of life to those
> who embrace her; happy are those who hold her tightly.
> Proverbs 3:13-18 NLT

Compose a prayer to ask for God's wisdom

_____

_____

_____

_____

_____

_____

_____

_____

_____

_____

_____

_____

_____

_____

_____

_____

_____

_____

Notes

Wielding Favor and Glory

Read chapter 8 of *Fight Like a Girl* and view DVD session 7.

Women do not hold the position of first created, but we hold the honor of being the crowning finale.

Insight

Nothing we do can separate us from the love of God–and nothing we do can make Him love us more. His love is a gracious gift that we don't deserve, but can boldly receive. In comparison to God, we are like the grass of the field that will dry up and blow away; but our holy, powerful, beautiful, almighty God bestows glory on us that rivals the most stunning flowers–and He values us infinitely.

LOCATE YOURSELF

Do I Bestow Favor and Glory?

Circle the underlined choice that best applies.

1. Do I <u>encourage</u> or <u>criticize</u> the people in my life?

2. Do I raise more <u>questions</u> or present more <u>answers</u>?

3. Do I see the contribution of <u>men</u> or <u>women</u> as more valuable?

4. Do I intentionally <u>raise</u> or <u>diminish</u> the people around me?

5. Are my words more often <u>tender</u> or <u>harsh</u>?

6. Am I more concerned with <u>beauty</u> or <u>order</u> in my home?

The woman is the glory of man.
1 Corinthians 11:7 NIV

1. What does it mean to be referenced as the "glory" as defined on pages 94- 95?

_____

_____

_____

_____

_____

_____

_____

2. In the above verse, the term *glory* defines a _____ dynamic between the man and the woman. (p. 94)

3. Pause here to list the men in your life who would be affected by your ability to transfer glory and honor.

_____   _____

_____   _____

_____   _____

_____   _____

All truth ultimately brings freedom. God never releases one group of people at the expense or to the detriment of another.

For man was not [created] from the woman, but woman from man;
neither was man created on account of or for the benefit of woman,
but woman on account of and for the benefit of man.
1 Corinthians 11:8-9 AMP

4. Women do not hold the position of first created. What position do we hold in the scheme of creation, and what is its significance?

_____

_____

_____

_____

_____

_____

_____

_____

_____

5. Why do you think the above passage has been distorted to label women as inferior to men? Have you ever heard it through the grid of this distortion?

_____

_____

_____

_____

_____

_____

_____

6. In light of this how do you feel about the comment "Men and women are equal, but not interchangeable"?

_____

_____

_____

_____

_____

_____

BIG *Idea*

Remembering the fact that the woman was created for the benefit of man reiterates the need men have for women. We have the potential to add value and meaning to every aspect of their lives. As women we are created in the *image* of God, but bear a different glory than that reflected by men.

7. In what ways are men and women equal? In what ways are they not interchangeable?

_____

_____

_____

_____

_____

_____

_____

_____

8. How do Paul's words that women were created for the benefit of men affect you? Do you feel demeaned by this truth or empowered by it?

_____

_____

_____

_____

_____

_____

_____

BIG *Idea*

Understand that everything in life is positioned by how you perceive it and the motive of your heart. If you believe the idea women were created for the benefit of men as derogatory then you will never see your value. I believe that Paul never meant to devalue women, but to give uniqueness to their place.

9. What does the mere presence of a woman often add to a man's life, be it father, husband, brother or son? (p. 97)

_____

_____

_____

_____

_____

_____

_____

_____

In this same way, husbands ought to love their wives as their own bodies. He who loves his wife loves himself. After all, no one ever hated his own body, but he feeds and cares for it, just as Christ does the church.
Ephesians 5:28-29 NIV

10. When men do not love and nurture women, do they hurt themselves? If so, how?

11. When women dishonor and disrespect men, what happens to their position?

12. How did you react to the imagery of women's ability to knight men? What did it awaken in you?

13. How can you use the "flat of the sword" to transfer honor and title? Have you been trying to use the "edge of the sword" to execute justice and judgment? If so, how? (pp. 99-100)

_____

_____

_____

_____

_____

_____

_____

14. Have you ever been publicly humiliated? Describe the situation. Choose today to intentionally bless the person who hurt you.

_____

_____

_____

_____

_____

_____

ACTIVITY

Write a script that you can use to begin speaking honor to the men in your life. Write a separate script that will transfer value to a fellow daughter.

For example: "I believe you are a man of God and that you always want to do what is right, just, and noble. And I am thankful that even when you make mistakes, you are not defined by them, but you always grow in the midst of them."

OR

"I so appreciate your ability to see beyond my failings and flaws to know the real heart of the issue. I am thankful that you do not judge me harshly, but you go deeper and pull the good out of me."

The man who finds a wife finds a treasure and receives favor from the Lord.
Proverbs 18:22 NLT

15. How do you feel about being called a treasure and a source of man's favor with God? How counterculture is this? How does our culture fight this truth?

_____

_____

_____

_____

_____

_____

_____

_____

_____

_____

_____

_____

_____

_____

_____

_____

_____

_____

_____

_____

_____

_____

BIG *Idea*

Most women are waiting for a knight in shining armor, though the Word of God indicates that women create the knight and make him worthy of the armor. This changes the women's role from one of passive waiting to one of proactivity.

God will carry out His decree of everlasting love and restore the correct order and positions of honor for His sons and daughters. We are seeing men and women the world over joining their strengths for the benefit of one another rather than wielding their power against one another. (p.103)

Make It Yours

Nothing changes when we behave according to how we have been treated. If we want to have something more in our lives and relationships, we must be something more. It is time for women to paint a new picture of the male-female dynamic. Below, journal this image.

_____

_____

_____

_____

_____

_____

_____

_____

_____

_____

_____

_____

_____

_____

_____

_____

_____

_____

_____

_____

_____

_____

_____

_____

_____

_____

_____

What Is the Power of Love?

Read chapter 9 of *Fight Like a Girl* and view DVD session 7.

To love and be loved is to feel the sun from both sides.
–David Viscott

Insight

God is love, and as His children, love is our gift from Him to enjoy among each other. Love is so powerful that it cannot fail, and its effects may be felt long beyond our earthly lives and interests. Love has the potential to swallow up every fear in our lives. God is healing His daughters so they can love fearlessly.

LOCATE YOURSELF

Am I Motivated by Feelings or Love?

1. I start to cry
   A. When watching an emotional television commercial.
   B. Not during commercials, but often during heartbreaking movies.
   C. When touched by a real-life situation.
   D. Only when peeling onions.

2. I will donate money
   A. To every cause that crosses my path.
   B. To most causes, if I have the money.
   C. Prayerfully and strategically.
   D. Never.

3. I have fallen in love
    A. Whenever I have met a godly man.
    B. A couple of times.
    C. Only once.
    D. Never.

SCORE
If you chose mostly As, instead of letting your emotions control you, let the love of God lead.
If you chose mostly Bs, you are sensitive to your emotions. Be careful to guard your heart.
If you chose mostly Cs, way to let the love and direction of God reign in your heart! Keep following His leading.
If you chose mostly Ds, your walls will hinder your walk with God and all He has for you. Go before Him in prayer.

> *Your eyes saw my unformed body. All the days ordained for me*
> *were written in your book before one of them came to be.*
> Psalm 139:16 NIV

1. Do you feel you were cast in a role you never auditioned for? As a daughter, what story do you want your life to tell? As a mother, what legacy do you want to leave behind for your children? What would your love story sound like?

_____

_____

_____

_____

_____

_____

_____

_____

_____

BIG *Idea*

Please realize that the end of your story is not written. Even now you are crafting your tale with your words and choices. Often what speaks to you the most profoundly on an emotional level is an area of your greatest longing.

2. Which recent movies have profoundly affected or defined love for you? In what ways?

_____

_____

_____

_____

_____

_____

3. Submission can be defined as "strength giving place to strength." Do you agree with this definition? Why or why not?

_____

_____

_____

_____

BIG *Idea*

Ideally, when we submit, our weaknesses are compensated for and our assets are maximized. Women do not yield to men because we are weak. It takes as much strength to follow as to lead. We see this exemplified in the life of Christ. He submitted all to the Father not because He was weak, but because in doing so His strengths were maximized.

4. In light of the above truth, in what areas of your life have you resisted and resented submitting because you felt doing so declared you weak?

_____

_____

_____

_____

_____

BIG *Idea*

Submission is a choice, a yielding of our will. It is never to be taken by force Women are exhorted to submit to their husbands because their husbands have pledged their lives to love, protect, and provide for their wives.

Submission is about protection. When we submit to God and resist Satan, he flees. Submission for women should never make them weaker, but rather position them for greater strength. (p. 109)

5. Are you better acquainted with your weaknesses or your strengths? Why?

_____

_____

_____

_____

_____

_____

_____

_____

_____

_____

_____

6. Which area of your life do you seek to protect—your weaknesses or your strengths?

_____

_____

_____

_____

7. According to this chapter, in what area is the woman most vulnerable?

_____

_____

_____

8. In what area is the man most vulnerable?

_____

_____

_____

9. According to Proverbs 31, what is the woman the guardian of?

_____

_____

_____

BIG *Idea*

Once love is openly declared, there is no going back. This happens between a man and a woman as well as between Christ and His beloved bride. For with Him, there is no stepping back from the promise of the love that propelled Him to risk all. (p. 110)

If I...have not love, I am nothing.
1 Corinthians 13:2 NIV

10. Discuss the following in the light of the above truth:
    A. Sex without love
    B. Money without love
    C. Relationships without love
    D. Family without love

11. What is the greatest enemy of love?

_____

_____

_____

_____

_____

There is no fear in love; but perfect love casts out fear.
1 John 4:18 NKJV

12. In what areas of your life or marriage have you been afraid to love fearlessly?

_____

_____

_____

_____

_____

13. What happens when women begin to love fearlessly? What are we promised? (p. 112)

_____

_____

_____

_____

14. How do we lift others? (p. 113)

_____

_____

_____

_____

_____

15. Explain the difference between denying a problem and strengthening a weakness. (p. 113)

_____

_____

_____

_____

> **Those from among you shall build the old waste places; you shall raise up the foundations of many generations; and you shall be called the Repairer of the Breach, the Restorer of Streets to Dwell In.**
> Isaiah 58:12 NKJV

16. In light of Isaiah 58:12, what characteristics might someone with the title of Repairer and Restorer have?

_____

_____

_____

_____

17. God is asking you to rise up and be among those who rebuild what has been lost. Utilizing Proverbs 14:1 as a guideline, what are some practical ways you can do this?

18. How might you "open your mouth with wisdom" and "have a tongue governed by the law of kindness," according to Proverbs 31:26

19. What are some ways wise women are a gift to their culture? (p. 115)

20. On our childhood playgrounds, how did the boys position themselves relationally? How did the girls?

21. In what areas in life has your husband, brother or friend asked you to lend strength to his weakness?

Make It Yours

Journal about what it might look like to lend your strength in the following areas:
  1. The life of your husband
  2. The life of your children and family
  3. The life of your friends
  4. Your own life

_____

_____

_____

_____

_____

_____

_____

_____

_____

_____

_____

_____

_____

_____

_____

_____

_____

_____

_____

_____

_____

_____

_____

_____

_____

Two with One Heart

Read chapter 10 of *Fight Like a Girl* and view DVD session 8.

**A great marriage is not when the "perfect couple" comes together. It is when an imperfect couple learns to enjoy their differences.
–Dave Meurer**

Insight

The dynamics of love, respect, protection, and honor are more than just keys to a successful marriage and intimate relationship. They are timeless principles with the ability to restore something crucial that was lost by both males and females–the power of dominion.

**The heavens are the Lord's heavens,
but the earth has He given to the children of men.**
Psalm 115:16 AMP

1. Define *dominion*. (p. 122)

_____

_____

_____

_____

_____

_____

2. Over what are we given dominion?

_____

_____

_____

_____

_____

_____

3. What is the difference between *dominion* and *domination*?

_____

_____

_____

_____

_____

> And God blessed them and told them, "Multiply and fill the earth
> and subdue it; you are masters of the fish and birds and all the animals.
> And look! I have given you the seed-bearing plants throughout the earth,
> and all the fruit trees for your food...." Then God looked over all
> that he had made, and it was excellent in every way.
> Genesis 1:28-31 TLB

4. What one thing did God not give Adam and Eve dominion over?

_____

_____

_____

5. What did God call the man and woman together?

_____

_____

_____

6. What is healthy authority or dominion given for?

_____

_____

_____

_____

_____

_____

_____

7. Why are authority figures or systems set in place?

_____

_____

_____

_____

_____

_____

_____

_____

_____

_____

_____

BIG *Idea*

Man is not the boss, with the woman *doing for him*. He is the leader who *does with her*. The husband needs to exercise his gift of naming and calling his wife "necessary". This causes the woman to be uniquely empowered to provide whatever he lacks. (p. 124)

8. What is reflected in the wife and children if the husband misuses his authority?

_____

_____

_____

_____

_____

_____

9. What does it look like when a woman misuses her influence? (p. 124)

_____

_____

_____

_____

_____

10. What is the power of two with one heart? (p. 124)

_____

_____

_____

_____

_____

_____

> **Fear not, for I have redeemed you;**
> **I have summoned you by name; you are mine.**
> Isaiah 43:1 NIV

11. Do the men in your life call you beautiful, wise, and necessary? If not, do you know there is One who calls you all of the above and more?

_____

_____

_____

_____

_____

_____

> **"The Lord will call you back as if you were a wife deserted and distressed**
> **in spirit–a wife who married young, only to be rejected," says your God.**
> Isaiah 54:6 NIV

12. In light of how sensitive God is to the plight of wounded and rejected women, do you believe the earth trembles at their mistreatment? If so, why?

_____

_____

_____

_____

_____

_____

ACTIVITY

Look at a map and discuss the areas of the world where the earth itself is unstable and where the daughters are mistreated. See how much of a correlation there is.

13. How does it make you feel to know that God cares so deeply about the injustices we face?

_____

_____

_____

_____

_____

_____

14. Why do you think the countries that violate the rights of women are suffering politically?

_____

_____

_____

_____

_____

_____

15. What is God's response to barren, unloved women? (p. 127)

_____

_____

_____

_____

_____

_____

My purpose is to give life in all its fullness.
John 10:10 NLT

16. What is the offspring of domination? (p. 127)

_____

_____

_____

_____

_____

_____

_____

The Son of Man came to seek and to save what was lost.
Luke 19:10

17. Why do both of the above verses illustrate so much more than life after death?

_____

_____

_____

_____

_____

_____

18. What was lost in the fall? (p. 128)

_____

_____

_____

_____

_____

_____

19. Do the above verses give us hope for our marriages?

_____

_____

_____

_____

_____

_____

BIG *Idea*

Redemption has the power to restore all that was lost in the transgression of the Fall. The Fall not only separated us from the presence of God; we also found ourselves troubled in the company of each other. If redemption was powerful enough to restore our relationship with God, it is certainly compelling enough to reconcile us to each other. Restoration begins as we submit to the truth of God's Word and consciously choose to do it His way. (p. 129)

In marriage, the right of women is love. The right of man is respect.

20. What are the two things that cause God to disregard prayers and offerings? (p. 131)

_____

_____

21. Think about your friends. Are you surrounded by women who bash men? Would you want your husband to keep company with men who spoke about women the way your friends speak about men?

_____

_____

_____

_____

_____

_____

_____

Pray about the relationships you have and allow God to strengthen the ones that affirm your marriage and separate you from the ones that don't.

22. What is more threatening to the health of a marriage—the storms within it or those that buffet it from the outside? (p. 138)

_____

_____

_____

_____

_____

_____

_____

Make It Yours

God always planned for our marriages to be banquets of joy and love, not some duty or obligation. God hates it when couples divorce each other—emotionally as well as legally. He wants our marriages to be gardens of support and affection where both parties draw strength from each other. He wants our children raised in an atmosphere of love and laughter.

In light of this truth, journal a picture of what you want your marriage or relationships to look like one month, three months, and six months from now.

_____

_____

_____

_____

_____

_____

_____

_____

_____

_____

_____

_____

_____

_____

_____

_____

_____

_____

_____

_____

_____

_____

_____

Notes

Fighting for Beauty

Read chapter 11 of *Fight Like a Girl* and view DVD session 9.

Beauty connects us with our deeper human longing...
a desperate cry for love.

Insight

We all want to be beautiful and to surround ourselves with beauty. We want to experience beauty's embrace in all we see, touch, taste, and smell. We long to see transformation and makeovers on every level. God originated our pursuit of beauty as well as our desire to see it realized.

He has made everything beautiful in its time.
Ecclesiastes 3:11 NIV

TEST YOURSELF

Am I Beautiful?

1. I believe the desire to be beautiful is a valid need.
   True or False

2. I tell myself beauty is unimportant, yet I spend a lot of time pursuing it.
   True or False

3. I see myself as beautiful.
   True or False

4. I often think that if I fix my physical "flaws," I will be happy.
   True or False

5. Beauty is for everyone.
   True or False

SCORE
If you chose more true than false, you are well on your way to realizing beauty.
If you chose more false than true, your beauty goes much deeper than you think.

---

1. Do you believe the drive for a makeover is wrong? Why or why not?

   _____

   _____

   _____

   _____

   _____

   _____

   _____

   _____

BIG *Idea*

God created within us an abiding hope that the old would somehow be made new—not that the old would become young. To be young again is not enough. Our destiny is pregnant with something no mortal eyes have seen: something, therefore, we can scarcely hope to believe exists. (p. 141)

2. What qualifies us for God's most extreme makeover, in which the old is made new?
   (1 Corinthians 2:9 and p. 142)

   _____

   _____

   _____

   _____

   _____

He has also set eternity in the hearts of men; yet they cannot
fathom what God has done from beginning to end.
Ecclesiastes 3:11 NIV

3. Who is in charge of driving our makeover?

_____

_____

_____

_____

_____

_____

_____

_____

_____

_____

_____

BIG *Idea*

God placed eternity in our hearts to cause us to look beyond this moment and live for a time and place yet unseen. Death is an uncomfortable fit for the sons and daughters of Adam and Eve. We do not wear its corruption well. It is, in fact, our enemy. It is only right that we would fight death and destruction and the theft of beauty on every front. (p. 144)

The path of the righteous is like the first gleam of the dawn,
shining ever brighter till the full light of day.
Proverbs 4:18 NIV

4. How accurately does Proverbs 4:18 describe the life of most Christians?

_____

_____

_____

_____

_____

_____

5. What is the difference between the way humans and animals respond to death? (p. 147)

_____

_____

_____

_____

_____

_____

6. What is the last enemy that will be destroyed? (p. 147)

_____

_____

_____

_____

_____

_____

_____

> When the perishable has been clothed with the imperishable, and
> the mortal with immortality, then the saying that is written
> will come true: "Death has been swallowed up in victory."
> 1 Corinthians 15:54 NIV

7. How is our makeover flipped inside out? (p. 150)

_____

_____

_____

_____

_____

_____

ACTIVITY
Leader: Get a ball of yarn or string.

Stand in a circle with one foot distance between each lady. While holding the end of the yarn, have one person toss the ball of yarn to another. As she tosses, she mentions a specific characteristic that she loves about the woman she tossed the yarn to. The woman who received the compliment will then toss to a different woman and mention a specific characteristic she admires about the new recipient of the ball of yarn. Keep going until each receives admiration and you form a connected web of yarn.

Therefore we do not lose heart. Though outwardly we are wasting away, yet inwardly we are being renewed day by day.
2 Corinthians 4:16 NIV

8. Why are women (both young and old) so incessantly harassed to empty themselves of all that is valuable and focus solely on the external?

9. How does the world describe Christian women?

10. What would be a more flattering description of a woman?

_____

_____

_____

_____

_____

_____

_____

_____

11. What should a Christian woman look like? How should she act? How should she dress? What should her voice sound like? (Feel free to use either pictures or words to describe.)

_____

_____

_____

_____

_____

_____

_____

12. Even though we will each experience the ultimate makeover when we die, are you ready to let Him call you beautiful now? Take a minute to read the following passage in light of the beauty of God's daughters.

_____

_____

_____

_____

_____

_____

_____

> **The king is enthralled by your beauty;**
> **honor him, for he is your lord.**
> Psalm 45:11 NIV

13. Is it difficult for you to imagine a king being enthralled by your beauty? For most of us it is. Take a moment to ask Him to reveal this truth to the most intimate places of your life.

_____

_____

_____

_____

_____

_____

_____

_____

BIG *Idea*

I see a generation of daughters so terrifying to the Enemy that he will do whatever he can in his power to distort your image, pervert your beauty, and rob you of your strength and power. He is the father of lies and speaks to you through a glass but darkly. But the Father of Light longs to speak to you face-to-face. He wants to touch the dark places where the wounding is so deep and severe it threatens to define your very existence. Ask, and He will allow you to behold Him. He will reach beyond the glass and call you altogether lovely and His own. (pp. 151-152)

14. How do we honor our Lord when it comes to the issue of beauty? (p. 152)

_____

_____

_____

_____

_____

_____

_____

_____

_____

_____

_____

Make It Yours

Think about the voices and phrases which condemn our authentic beauty and write God's corresponding word that attacks that fallacy. Also, collect pictures of women who look like a comfortable fit of who you are, not who you are told to be.

Daughter, you are altogether lovely.

Flawed but Authentic

Read chapter 12 of *Fight Like a Girl* and view DVD session 9.

We prove our authenticity by our reaction and responses to our enemies.

Insight

I am sure you know being fake will not get us where we need to go. I am also certain that you find in yourself a persistent hunger for something else. There is a longing in each of us for a dynamic that encompasses the realm of something deeper and more enduring….the authentic.

TEST YOURSELF

Am I Authentic?

(0=I've never done this; 5=I've often done this)

1. I say what's on my mind even if I know it will offend others.
0 1 2 3 4 5

2. I complain because I don't like to pretend everything is perfect.
0 1 2 3 4 5

3. I don't go to church when I feel guilty about something I've done.
0 1 2 3 4 5

4. I offer to pray for people even when I know I won't.
0 1 2 3 4 5

5. Even if I'm in a bad mood, I act happy to please others.
0 1 2 3 4 5

SCORE
0-7: You are being true to your life purpose. Continue to live authentically, but don't be afraid to be realistic about your struggles.
8-15: Your honesty is commendable. Remember your identity in Christ and be an authentic woman of God.
16-25: You are mistaking authenticity for "real" and perhaps even carnality. Get ready for some clarity.

1. Why is flawless, controlled beauty less appealing than imperfect, wild beauty?

_____

_____

_____

_____

_____

_____

_____

2. Do you think women today are ready for something more than the silk-flower version of their present Christian reality? Do you think they have settled for the unreal because they're afraid to hope for something more? If so, why are they afraid?

_____

_____

_____

_____

_____

_____

3. Give the definition of *real*. (p. 164) Give the definition of *authentic*. (p. 164) What is the major difference between *authentic* and *real*?

_____

_____

_____

_____

_____

_____

_____

4. Are people being authentic when they share every feeling or thought they have? How can women find balance between being vulnerable through authenticity and being inconsiderate through their desire to "tell it like it is"?

_____

_____

_____

_____

_____

_____

_____

_____

_____

_____

_____

_____

_____

_____

_____

_____

BIG *Idea*

Sisters, you have no obligation whatsoever to do what your sinful nature urges you to do. For if you keep on following it, you will perish. But if through the power of the Holy Spirit you turn from it and its evil deeds, you will live. For all who are led by the Spirit of God are children of God.

Romans 8:12-14 NLT
(author paraphrase)

The ability to live over and above our immediate emotional dictates and reactions (regardless of hormonal fluctuations) is a God-given, Spirit-breathed gift of grace.

> Bless those who curse you, pray for those who mistreat you. If someone
> strikes you on one cheek, turn to him the other also. If someone
> takes your cloak, do not stop him from taking your tunic.
> Luke 6:28-29 NIV

5. The above verses give the *authentic* response to mistreatment. What is the *real* response?

_____

_____

_____

_____

_____

_____

_____

_____

6. What is one way we are privileged to model God's behavior when we're mistreated, misjudged, or slandered? (p. 159)

_____

_____

_____

_____

_____

_____

_____

_____

> Love your enemies! Pray for those who persecute you! In that way,
> you will be acting as true [authentic] children of your Father in heaven.
> For he gives his sunlight to both the evil and the good,
> and he sends rain on the just and on the unjust, too.
> Matthew 5:44-45 NLT

7. What does this passage tell us about authenticity? Does authenticity vary or is it consistent?

_____

_____

_____

_____

_____

8. Authentic individuals are the _____ no matter where they are. (p. 159)

9. As a general rule, the more refined the object, the more care in its treatment. Returning to the example of a woman as crystal, what does this say about your value? Is it always wrong to be more fragile?

_____

_____

_____

_____

_____

> **Husbands, likewise, dwell with them with understanding, giving honor to the wife, as to the weaker vessel, and as being heirs together of the grace of life, that your prayers may not be hindered.**
> 1 Peter 3:7 NKJV

10. When you have read this verse before, did you put the emphasis on the concept the "weaker vessel" or on "being heirs together"? What does the verse say about the way God protects his daughters? (p. 161)

_____

_____

_____

_____

_____

Two elderly women met at a party.
"My dear," said the first woman, "are those real pearls?"
"They are," replied the second woman.
"Of course the only way I could know for sure would be for
me to bite them," explained the first woman.
The second responded, "Yes, but for that you would need
real teeth."

11. List the characteristics of diamonds. List the characteristics of cubic zirconium. Which would you rather have: a flawed, authentic diamond or a massive, man-made cubic zirconium?

_____

_____

_____

_____

_____

_____

_____

Beauty is truth, truth beauty.
–John Keats

12. Think about, or discuss, the above quote in light of our culture's paradigm of "beauty is reality and reality is beauty." (p. 165)

_____

_____

_____

_____

_____

_____

13. What is the difference between *reality* and *truth*? (pp. 165-166)

14. On what three levels do people hear things? (p. 167)

15. What is the connection between *authentic* and *original*? (p. 168)

16. In relation to the discussion of pantyhose, are there any neutral accessories or items of clothing you feel compelled to wear or not wear to conform to Christianity's standards?

17. When we do something we really don't want to do but that we know is right, are we being fake?

_____

_____

_____

_____

_____

_____

_____

_____

_____

18. Have you ever felt pressured to appear perfect? Where did that pressure come from?

BIG *Idea*

To be authentic or genuine, we don't have to be flawless! Our flaws actually declare us authentic. In fact, if we represent ourselves as flawless, then we most certainly declare ourselves as fake. No one is perfect or good, save God. (p. 163)

_____

_____

_____

_____

_____

_____

_____

_____

Make It Yours

Do you realize there is something unique and original about you? How can you be who God forged you to be?

_____

_____

_____

_____

_____

_____

_____

_____

_____

_____

_____

_____

_____

_____

_____

_____

_____

_____

_____

_____

_____

_____

_____

_____

_____

_____

_____

_____

_____

Notes

Fighting with Accessories

Read chapter 13 of *Fight Like a Girl* and view DVD session 9.

Everything of beauty is birthed through the process of fire.

Insight

Fire makes us pure. Fire separates the precious from the vile and makes the hidden apparent. As impurities bubble up and dance on the surface, there is a decision to be made: Do we leave them or let them be removed?

---

1. Revisiting the rock-polisher dynamic, what was the difference between an amethyst jewel and a purple stone destined for a keychain? (pp. 171-172)

_____

_____

_____

_____

_____

_____

_____

_____

_____

_____

115

2. What areas of life have you limited God to polishing the rock rather than faceting?

_____

_____

_____

_____

_____

_____

_____

_____

_____

_____

_____

_____

_____

_____

_____

_____

_____

> # BIG *Idea*
>
> The truth is, most women like jewels and jewelry. We are supposed to. I did not say we are to lust after jewelry or trust in our accessories as an accurate measure of our worth; but rather each daughter has a God-given appreciation for the beauty of jewels. Why else would God hide such a multitude of various and precious stones within the earth if not for His children to unearth and enjoy? (pp. 173-174)

3. Why do you think women are so attracted to beautiful jewelry?

_____

_____

_____

_____

_____

_____

_____

_____

4. What does the abundance and diversity of jewels on earth say about God? How does that make you feel about God?

_____

_____

_____

_____

_____

Then they mounted four rows of precious stones on it. In the first row there was a ruby, a topaz and a beryl; in the second row a turquoise, a sapphire and an emerald; in the third row a jacinth, an agate and an amethyst; in the fourth row a chrysolite, an onyx and a jasper. They were mounted in gold filigree settings. There were twelve stones, one for each of the names of the sons of Israel, each engraved like a seal with the name of one of the twelve tribes.
Exodus 39:10-14 NIV

5. Why do you think God chose twelve different stones to represent the twelve tribes of Israel? How does the way they were set declare their value?

_____

_____

_____

_____

_____

"They shall be Mine," says the LORD of hosts, "On the day that I make them My jewels. And I will spare them as a man spares his own son who serves him." Then you shall again discern between the righteous and the wicked, between one who serves God and one who does not serve Him.
Malachi 3:17-18 NKJV

6. How does God make us His jewels?

_____

_____

_____

_____

_____

_____

_____

_____

_____

> I will bring that group through the fire and make them pure,
> just as gold and silver are refined and purified by fire. They will
> call on my name, and I will answer them. I will say, "These
> are my people," and they will say, "The Lord is our God."
> Zechariah 13:9 NLT

7. What does fire separate? (p. 175)

_____

_____

_____

_____

_____

_____

_____

_____

_____

> Behold, I have refined you, but not as silver;
> I have tested you in the furnace of affliction.
> Isaiah 48:10 NKJV

8. Who you are in the fire is who you are. How do you feel about this statement? Do you think how you respond in the hard places in life are an accurate measurement of who you are?

_____

_____

_____

_____

BIG *Idea*

Fire does not just reveal what is flawed; it reveals what is beautiful as well. Who would have imagined colors ranging from the aqua of water to the blue of the sky could be coaxed from brown? (p. 176)

_____

_____

_____

_____

_____

_____

_____

9. Because most gemstones are mined, what is the environment that forges them? (p. 178)

_____

_____

_____

_____

_____

_____

_____

BIG *Idea*

There is something of beauty to be learned from every dark and lonely place in our lives. It is in those times of obedience during suffering that we have an opportunity to experience our Father as more than enough. Out of the rough material of our trials, He is more than willing to fashion objects of beauty. (p. 178)

10. Tell about a difficult season or time in your life that brought beauty in the next season. While you were in the midst of the process, did it feel like beauty could ever come of it? Why or why not? How does this knowledge prepare you for future trials?

_____

_____

_____

_____

_____

_____

_____

_____

_____

_____

11. Which would you prefer, a two-carat diamond that is off-color, unsymmetrical, and visibly flawed or a one-carat, symmetrical, colorless diamond that appears flawless to the naked eye?

_____

_____

_____

_____

_____

_____

_____

_____

_____

I delight greatly in the Lord; my soul rejoices in my God. For he
has clothed me with garments of salvation and arrayed me in a robe
of righteousness, as a bridegroom adorns his head like a priest,
and as a bride adorns herself with her jewels.

Isaiah 61:10 NIV

ACTIVITY

Go through a magazine such as *In Style* or *Bride* that has a wide selection of fine jewelry (precious and semiprecious stones and/or pearls). Pick a set you would want to adorn yourself with as a bride.

OR

Have each woman bring to the group her most precious piece of jewelry. Share with the group why it is special to her (e.g., "This was given to me by my grandmother, husband, etc.")

12. Look back over the past year. Have you been shorting yourself of beautiful accessories which will last a lifetime? If so, why? Were you afraid of the process required to receive them?

_____

_____

_____

_____

_____

_____

_____

_____

_____

_____

_____

_____

_____

_____

_____

_____

Make It Yours

The revelation of fire usually occurs in the secret place of our heart. Often we will be in prayer when God points out the impurities He longs to redeem as beautiful.

What areas of pain and frustration will you believe God to make into an object of beauty? Write about these areas and take them to prayer.

"Fight Like A Girl has given me the confidence I need to get past the lie that I don't measure up in a man's world. Now I understand that women have influence that is unique to who we are."

Fighting with Influence

14

Read chapter 14 of *Fight Like a Girl* and view DVD session 10.

**When God is with you, it really doesn't matter
what is in your hand...only that you use it.**

Insight

The day came when Deborah, the judge, was no longer content to sit and judge the conflicts among her own. To watch the hopeless infighting while a harsh and cruel enemy mocked their God and ravaged their cities. She had grown weary of the sound of mourning and despair and chose instead to sing.

---

1. Does anything ever change when all we do it sit around and judge? Why or why not?

_____

_____

_____

_____

_____

_____

_____

_____

_____

2. Though Deborah had complete authority, there was not a catalyst for change until a mother's heart woke within her. How does Deborah's life hold an urgent message and a call to awaken the women of our age?

_____

_____

_____

_____

_____

_____

_____

3. What was the political climate in Israel when Deborah became judge? (p. 183)

_____

_____

_____

_____

_____

_____

4. How long did she judge Israel before any true change in the nation was brought about? (p. 184)

_____

_____

_____

_____

_____

_____

_____

5. After reviewing the story of Deborah, has your romanticized view of her life been stripped away? How do you see her now?

_____

_____

_____

_____

_____

_____

6. Write about a quiet season when God was preparing you to battle in the next phase of your life.

_____

_____

_____

_____

_____

_____

> Deborah said to Barak, "The Lord, the God of Israel, commands you:
> 'Go and gather 10,000 men of Naphtali and Zebulun.
> Lead them to Mount Tabor.'"
> Judges 4:6 NCV

7. Notice again, Deborah removed herself from the equation and spoke as God's representative. How comfortable would you feel with this dynamic? How intimately is this tied to authority and leadership?

_____

_____

_____

_____

_____

8. Has your gender ever kept you from speaking the message God has given you? Has Deborah's life awakened boldness inside of you? If so, how will you respond?

_____

_____

_____

_____

_____

_____

_____

_____

_____

_____

BIG *Idea*

Whenever God begins to shift things, there is a sense of urgency. He appears to respond to years of our desperate prayers or outcries with a sudden move from inaction to action and interrupts our cycle of despair. If we are wise, we will allow this urgency to carry over to our responses in obedience to His call to action. (p. 185)

9. Give an example from your life when you knew God was asking for your obedience. How did you respond?

_____

_____

_____

_____

_____

_____

_____

_____

_____

_____

_____

_____

BIG *Idea*

God's command and promise stirred [Barak] enough to respond, but not enough to move him into action. He was afraid. He actually threatened to disobey the command of both his earthly ruler and his heavenly Ruler if [Deborah] did not accompany him. (p. 186)

10. Like Barak, has fear ever kept you from moving into action, even though your heart was willing and you knew it would be the best for everyone involved? What was the result?

_____

_____

_____

_____

_____

_____

_____

_____

_____

_____

_____

_____

11. What can we do to remind ourselves of the need to always be willing without being scared or paranoid?

_____

_____

_____

_____

_____

_____

_____

_____

_____

_____

BIG *Idea*

Deborah used her authority and influence to foster obedience in Barak. She did not try to pull her rank as a judge, or play her "God card" as prophetess and rebuke him for his defiance. She lent him her strength. All true leaders, whether male or female, need to lend their strength rather than pull rank. (p. 187)

12. Women of influence (i.e. leaders, mothers, employers), are you more concerned with getting the need met, the project done, or the proper respect due your rank? Why?

_____

_____

_____

_____

_____

_____

_____

13. Write about a time when someone of great influence spent his or her strength to change your life.

_____

_____

_____

"Of course I will go with you," Deborah answered "But you will not get credit for the victory. The Lord will let a woman defeat Sisera."
Judges 4:9 NCV

BIG *Idea*

You might be tempted to think Deborah was referring to gaining credit for the defeat of Sisera for herself, but she was not. Another woman was soon to come on the scene, Jael, who would finish the job Barak began. Perhaps Deborah's ability to see beyond the immediate circumstances was the very reason Barak valued her company. (p. 187)

14. Like Deborah, are you willing to see beyond present circumstances and take hold of God's plan?

_____

_____

_____

_____

_____

_____

_____

_____

Jael went out to meet Sisera. She said to him, "Come into my tent, master! Come in. Don't be afraid." So Sisera went into Jael's tent, and she covered him with a rug.
Judges 4:18 NCV

Sisera ran to a tent of alliance, thinking he would find safety but when God begins to turn tables, there is no safe place for the enemy. (p. 189)

But Jael, the wife of Heber, took a peg and a hammer. She quietly went to Sisera. Since he was very tired, he was sleeping. She hammered the tent peg through the side of Sisera's head and into the ground! And so Sisera died.
Judges 4:21 NCV

This woman understood when the Enemy comes into your home, you must take him out with whatever means are available. When the Enemy trespasses our domain, God will always use what is in our hands. He will anoint what we have already been faithful to wield.

"What is in your hand" means whatever is in your care or control. This could be money or possessions. It could be talents and abilities. What you withhold or refuse to give from your hand is often very revealing of what resides within your heart. (p. 194)

15. The name Jael means "value." She understood that what looked insignificant was actually invaluable. Are you ready to wield the weapon God has placed in your hand to defeat the Enemy?

_____

_____

_____

_____

_____

_____

_____

16. So, what is in your hand?

_____

_____

_____

_____

_____

_____

_____

_____

_____

ACTIVITY

Gather five random objects and take a minute to think of the many functions (ordinary and extraordinary) each has. Discuss how God could anoint each of these objects to defeat the Enemy.

Apply the principle of the above activity to your life. Ask God to reveal the things you have that can be used on a daily basis to lend strength to others and even defeat the Enemy. Write them down.

Make It Yours

Battles are won in the realm of the spirit long before they are ever finalized in the natural. You must allow God to settle it while you are on your knees before you can get the strength to stand before an enemy. You have to see the enemy defeated before you will ever gain the strength necessary to win. (p. 191)

What is in your hand? Does it seem too familiar to be of any value? How can God use it for His glory? How have you seen this happen already?

_____

_____

_____

_____

_____

_____

_____

_____

_____

_____

_____

_____

_____

_____

_____

_____

_____

_____

_____

_____

_____

_____

_____

Notes

The Power of the Moment 15

Read chapter 15 of *Fight Like a Girl* and view DVD session 11.

**Your past and your future intersect
in this moment called now.**

Insight

The choices we make in the now, whether for good or bad, exert incredible influence on our futures. We can actually make a conscientious choice today to not allow our pasts to dictate our choices, but there is no way we can stop our present choices from affecting our futures.

---

1. Does this frighten or empower you to realize the power your present choices exert on your future? Why?

_____

_____

_____

_____

_____

_____

_____

_____

2. In what way can you guard against allowing your past to dictate the present?

_____

_____

_____

_____

_____

_____

_____

_____

> **Now to him who is able to do immeasurably more than all we ask
> or imagine, according to his power that is at work within us.**
> Ephesians 3:20 NIV

3. When reviewing the Old Testament and the pending revelation of Christ, do you ever find yourself frustrated in the lack of power in the *now*? If so, how do you deal with this frustration?

_____

_____

_____

BIG *Idea*

What about now?...
My heart cries out in
the midst of His
goodness to see His
power. I want to see His hand
stretched forth into our now. I
believe God is asking his women
to cry out and ask for something
more... WHAT ABOUT NOW?
(p.199)

4. Reviewing Ephesians 3:20, what would "immeasurably more" look like in our now?

5. What areas in your life do you need God's power to become evident?

6. Are you content with the status quo and the way things are now? Why or why not? Are you willing to be that woman who cries out for something more for those around you? If so, how will you accomplish this?

7. Do you realize what an honor it is that God extends His power to work within us? How are you are limiting Him from using His full potential in you?

8. Have you ever tried to pick and choose the ways God could use your life? If so, describe the circumstances and the results.

_____

_____

_____

_____

_____

_____

9. Are you scared to ask for things totally out of the realm of your control? Have you ever been afraid to pursue a course of action because you didn't know whether God would come through? Describe the situation.

_____

_____

_____

_____

_____

_____

ACTIVITY
God is Calling You

> Spend some time in prayer as a group, asking God to reveal to you what He would like for you to accomplish. Make a commitment to each other and to God to pray for the ministry He calls you to and to walk along the path He directs as you continue praying about it.

Praise the Lord, O my soul; all my inmost being, praise his holy name. Praise the Lord, O my soul, and forget not all his benefits–who forgives all your sins and heals all your diseases, who redeems your life from the pit and crowns you with love and compassion, who satisfies your desires with good things so that your youth is renewed like the eagle's.

Psalm 103:1-5 NIV

BIG *Idea*

God is extravagant in His restoration. Not only does He redeem our lives from the pit; He crowns us with His love and compassion, satisfies our desires with good, and renews our youth! How could so much goodness be found in one breath? (p. 201)

10. Would you ever dream of not sharing God as Savior just because somebody did not respond to His invitation of salvation? So, why is it that we are afraid to call Him Healer (even though this is what He calls Himself) if somebody is not healed? Have you ever limited God in this area? Explain.

11. God is the One who tied forgiveness to healing. Why do we so easily separate them?

12. Who or what is waiting to be released when you speak forth God's Word?

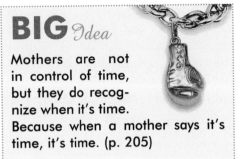

BIG *Idea*

Mothers are not in control of time, but they do recognize when it's time. Because when a mother says it's time, it's time. (p. 205)

The phrase "It's your time!" has been stirring in my spirit. Notice I did not say "It's your turn." When it's someone's turn, everyone else has to take a break and watch while they take center stage; but when it's time, everyone joins in! (pp. 205-206)

In the last days, God says, I will pour out my Spirit on all people. Your sons and daughters will prophesy, your young men will see visions, your old men will dream dreams.
Acts 2:17 NIV

13. List some of the things you think it is time for.

_____   _____
_____   _____
_____   _____
_____   _____
_____   _____
_____   _____
_____   _____

14. Can you believe it is possible that God has saved the best until now? What might this look like?

_____
_____
_____
_____
_____
_____
_____

Make It Yours

Is God stirring you to ask for something more than what you've seen? Have you been afraid to ask because you fear disappointment? Now is the time; now is your moment.

Notes

You Are Being Watched!

Read chapter 16 of *Fight Like a Girl* and view DVD session 12.

For all creation is waiting eagerly for that future day when God will reveal who his children really are.
–Romans 8:19 NLT

Insight

There are times when we know beyond a shadow of a doubt we are not only being watched, but we are on display and possibly being scored or judged.

1. What situations have you been in where your performance was being scrutinized? How did it feel? Does competition make you succeed or shut down? Explain.

_____

_____

_____

_____

_____

_____

_____

_____

2.   Have you ever been in a situation where you felt beaten before you began because of the perception of others?

_____

_____

_____

_____

_____

_____

3.   Do we perform differently when we are expected to win as opposed to being expected to fail? What does this look like for you with the season you are currently in?

_____

_____

_____

_____

_____

BIG *Idea*

The audience surrounding us is filled with joyful expectation. Creation is not even concerned with the possibility of our failure. We've already done that. As the descendants and seed of Adam, we were present and accounted for in him when creation was changed and subjected to this domain of useless ruin. When Jesus chose to lay down His life, everything was reversed and it all began to change again. (pp. 212-213)

4.   How does it make you feel to know the earth watches in joyful expectation, not in judgment? Why do you think creation has such hope in us?

_____

_____

_____

_____

_____

_____

_____

_____

_____

5. Isn't it amazing that God's redeeming power not only restored us to Himself but also recovered what was lost in the fall? Do you still see areas in your life that are not yet recovered? If so, what are they?

_____

_____

_____

_____

_____

_____

_____

_____

_____

> **Again, the gift of God is not like the result of the one man's sin: The judgment followed one sin and brought condemnation, but the gift followed many trespasses and brought justification. For if, by the trespass of the one man, death reigned through that one man, how much more will those who receive God's abundant provision of grace and of the gift of righteousness reign in life through the one man, Jesus Christ.**
> Romans 5:16-17 NIV

6. Referencing the above verse, what would our position "in Christ" look like? (p. 214)

_____

_____

_____

_____

_____

_____

_____

_____

BIG *Idea*

For two thousand years death has been losing its grip, and sooner than we know, it will all change.... We no longer live under the transgression of Adam but under the righteous reign of Jesus Christ. Creation no longer looks upon us with scorn and questioning. Creation looks on us with hope and with the understanding that the finality of death's reign is over. The old order has passed away, and the promise of the new stretches before us. The great exchange will take place and then the visible will be overtaken by the invisible, the mortal will be replaced by the immortal, and death itself will be swallowed up in victory. (pp. 213-214)

For what is seen is temporary, but what is unseen is eternal.
2 Corinthians 4:18 NIV

7. Since "temporary" is tied to time, could it be that time itself was created to highlight the story of redemption?

8. Death may reign in the realm of the seen, but Jesus reigns in the realm of the eternal. Do you know you have truly been freed and justified?

9. Are there areas of regret and disappointment in your life? Do you feel it will take a long time for those areas to be replaced with God's light?

_____

_____

_____

_____

_____

_____

_____

_____

_____

10. Don't you know the price of your sin was already paid? Do you realize you no longer have to be a guardian of shame? What difference will this knowledge make in your life?

_____

_____

_____

_____

_____

_____

_____

_____

_____

11. How can you daily walk out the realization that death does not reign in your life?

_____

_____

_____

_____

_____

_____

_____

_____

> It is written: "I believed; therefore I have spoken." With that same spirit of faith we also believe and therefore speak, because we know that the One who raised the Lord Jesus from the dead will also raise us with Jesus and present us with you in His presence.
>
> 2 Corinthians 4:13-14 NIV

12. Will you begin to receive the spirit of faith that speaks for the unseen and eternal? How will you start living differently and speak God's language of hope and love?

_____

_____

_____

_____

_____

_____

_____

Redemption is God's answer to mankind's failure!

13. Do you realize the end of the story is not about you and your accomplishments but instead it is all about Him? How will this truth cause you to approach life?

_____

_____

_____

_____

_____

_____

_____

_____

_____

_____

BIG *Idea*

Creation is not watching us, arms crossed, challenging us to impress it. Actually, it is nodding its approval and lifting its voice, saying, "You go, girl! Fight fearlessly the battle only you can win, and wield with strength again the weapons God entrusted to your care. You are the very one I have been watching for." (p. 217)

14. Do you place limitations on yourself? How would your life look if, in every area of your life, you began to connect with the Source who is so far from earthly limitation and confines?

15. How will you live your life as an empowered daughter of God? Will you begin to use the areas you have influence over to awaken others to their quest for more?

16. Each generation should walk in abundantly more freedom than the one before it. Are you willing to pay the price to go after this?

Make It Yours

Cover others with love.
Raise them with honor.
Empower them with wisdom.
Encourage them with vision.
Restore their dreams with purity.
Recover their strength with joy.

Free them with His truth.
Give them a future with legacy.
Awe them with beauty.
Inspire them with His splendor.
Stir them with holiness and passion.

LET THE UNVEILING BEGIN...

Ask the Holy Spirit to remove every drape of shame and cover you with another cape more outfitted to who you are.

Cry out for the unveiling of My daughter. She must be revealed, released, and freed to both respond and be responded to. Your unveiling is at hand. (p. 221)

What areas of life is God speaking to you about? Where do you need to lavish love and freely receive it.

_____

_____

_____

_____

_____

_____

_____

_____

_____

_____

_____

_____

_____

_____

_____

united states
PO BOX 888
PALMER LAKE, CO 80133-0888

800.648.1477 *us and canada
T:719.487.3000
F:719.487.3300

mail@messengerintl.org

For **more** information
please contact **us:**

europe
PO BOX 622
NEWPORT, NP19 8ZJ
UNITED KINGDOM

44(0) 870.745.5790
F:44(0) 870.745.5791

europe@messengerintl.org

WOMEN:
Join Lisa Bevere's **ENGAGE** program.

Visit us online at www.messengerintl.org

australia
PO BOX 6200
DURAL, D.C. NSW 2158
AUSTRALIA

IN AUS: 1.300.650.577
+61.2.8850.1725
F:+61 2.8850.1735

aus@messengerintl.org

Books by Lisa

Fight Like a Girl
Kissed the Girls and Made Them Cry
Be Angry, But Don't Blow It!
Out of Control and Loving It!
The True Measure of a Woman
You Are Not What You Weigh

Fight Like *a* Girl
The Power of Being a Woman

Curriculum Includes

12 Sessions on 4 DVD's
Hardback Book and Interactive Workbook
Makeup Bag
Bracelet

Why is it that women often don't like women? What could possibly cause a large portion of us to reject our own gender? More often than not we lack an appreciation for women. We associate men with strength and women with weakness. We therefore attempt life in roles as men, only to find ourselves conflicted. But God is awakening and empowering His daughters to realize who they truly are, as well as their unique and significant contributions.

 *bringing healing to women of all ages.*

THE KISSED GIRLS AND THEM MADE CRY

CURRICULUM INCLUDES
12 SESSIONS ON 3 DVD'S, BOOK,
INTERACTIVE WORKBOOK, MAKEUP BAG
BONUS Q&A DVD

Don't believe the lie—sexual purity isn't about rules...it's about freedom and power. It is time to take back what we've cheaply given away. The *Kissed the Girls and Made Them Cry* kit is not only designed for youth but also for women of all ages who long for a greater intimacy with Jesus and need to embrace God's healing and restoring love.

"I'm 15. and through your kit my nightmare has been turned back to a dream!"

Beautiful -DVD

Part of being beautiful and authentic is realizing the value of you, the original! An original is the beginning of something. You were never meant to be defined by others and reduced to a pseudo copy or forgery. Do you know there is something extremely unique and beautiful only you have? Whether you embrace your uniqueness or live out your life as only a mixed blend of the lives of others is really up to you. But know this - the whole world is watching in the hope that you will be a beautiful original.

Life Without Limits -DVD

It is definitely no longer about us, but about Him! God is calling a generation of women who are willing to take risks and go out over their heads in Him. Women brave enough to trust Him with every area of their life. He is watching for wild women who will be reckless in both their abandonment to God and their commitment to obedience. It is time to embrace His freedom in every area. This powerful and dynamic video was recorded at a women's mentoring conference and will empower you in these crucial areas:
- Completing versus competing
- Making your marriage a place of power
- Refining and defining your motivation
- Harnessing your power of influence
- Answering the mandate

Extreme Makeover -2 CD SET

Makeovers of every kind are the current craze. Not only are faces and bodies being hauled over, but everything is subject to this before-and-after experimentation. People just can't seem to get enough, and rather than judging, the church needs to ask the all-important question…Why? I believe it is because we are all desperate for change!

It's Time -CD

For too long we have had the attitude, "It's my turn!" But when God begins to pour out His spirit, it is nobody's turn, it becomes everybody's time. It is time for God's gifts in His body to come forth. The Father is gifting men and women alike to shine in each and every realm of life. Discover what He has placed in your hand and join the dance of a lifetime.